GRAND ILLUSIONS

new country

GRAND ILLUSIONS
new country

IDEAS AND PRACTICAL PROJECTS FOR
CONTEMPORARY COUNTRY STYLE

NICK RONALD AND DAVID ROBERTS

Trafalgar Square Publishing

This book is dedicated to dear Tiggs (David's mother),

who celebrates her eightieth birthday this year.

First published in the United States of America in 2000 by

Trafalgar Square Publishing

North Pomfret, Vermont 05053

Color separation by Colorlito S.r.l. in Milan, Italy
Printed and bound in Singapore by Tien Wah Press

Text © Nick Ronald and David Roberts, 2000

ISBN 1-57076-158-2

Library of Congress Catalog Card Number: 99-69295

Editor: Emma Callery
Art Director: Meryl Lloyd
Designer: Alison Shackleton
Photographers: Caroline Arber, David Downie and Andrew Wood
Photographic stylists: Meryl Lloyd and Nick Ronald

Please note that the paint names quoted throughout this book relate to
Grand Illusions' own range of new generation water-based paints. They
are available by mail order. See pages 140-141 for the addresses of
Grand Illusions and other stockists of water-based paints.

contents

introduction

Welcome to Grand Illusions' New Country, for what we hope will be a refreshing departure into a world where simplicity takes the place of swags, sophistication replaces sentimentality and modern is neither minimal nor a forbidden territory.

This book is dedicated to all those people for whom the very term 'country style' evokes a cringe or grimace. It is, after all, a much-plundered description that covers a multitude of styles or sins (depending upon your viewpoint), and it's time to move on.

New Country is a place where decorating is likely to be inspired by nature and warmed by the use of natural elements. It is the perfect antidote to this frenetic, busy, dot.com world, where we seem to be rushing lemming-like into a high-tech abyss. To those who subscribe, it's goodbye to heavily laden dressers of bric-a-brac, adios to those colors inspired by our forefathers and a big hello to a fresh and relaxed decorating style.

We made the move to the countryside nearly two years ago, and while we may miss some of the suburban culture, life in the country has been a revelation. It is the genuine warmth of the people, their practicality, their generosity and their welcoming spirit – it is to those people that this book is really dedicated.

Nick Ronald and David Roberts

as nature intended

Even though the following philosophy might make most men run a mile, modern decorating or interior design is now a rather more sensual affair, a touchy-feely sort of thing. Long gone are the days when all it took was two coats of trade emulsion (latex) paint, although that could still be the starting point, and one amazing leap into a new era.

Decorating today is all about how your rooms make you feel – a veritable feast for all the senses. Obviously, sight is enhanced through the use of color, light and style; then touch is suggested by the creation of different textures; smell by the use of aromatherapy, scented candles and fresh flowers, and hearing and taste by your choice of the rich variety of music and food that is now available. A heady mix if ever there was one, but one to which you really do need to subscribe fully if you are ever to make it across the frontiers of New Country.

New Country is also about simplicity and a vaguely romantic view that embraces a mix of eclecticism and elegance, always tempered with restraint. New Country is organic in its use of texture and natural materials and in its appreciation of nature and the changing seasons and how they affect our homes. As ever, it is inspired by travels at home and abroad – these experiences provide an irreplaceable sub-conscious directory to which we refer daily.

Be warned though ... decorating New Country style is not a purist discipline, nor meant to be. We err on the side of a relaxed and informal style, neither confined by tradition nor phased by fashion. Comfort reigns high on the list of necessities and, above all, you do not need to live in the country to subscribe. Cast your eyes over these pages and soak up the abundance found within them.

an inspired choice

Sources of inspiration are an incredibly personal affair and we are always being asked what inspires us. There is no doubt, of course, that what inspires one person, might leave another completely cold, but it is these experiences that are the cornerstone of our success. For what it's worth, here are some of our favorite places, people and things.

Not surprisingly, the cities of Barcelona and Paris are high on the list — both are cities of passion and have a vibrance that is almost hedonistic. Barcelona offers a fusion of wonderful architecture old and new, Gaudi and Miro, and outstanding restaurants with simple Catalan cuisine and inspiring interiors. Paris is a city of incredible romance, various cultures and, again, inspiring shops — and is also home to FNAC, probably the most state-of-the-art music retailer in the world and a must for anyone who wishes an international collection of music.

Antwerp is possibly less obvious and one of the best kept secrets. Here you can find brilliant architecture, excellent food and beer and some of the most inspiring shops in

Europe where different product groups are divided into areas or streets. The antique section is remarkable and very unusual, as is the interior design street, which is home to Flammand and one of the best florists in Europe. Similarly impressive is the Home & Garden Fair in Amsterdam. This fair takes place every May in the grounds of a large country house just outside Amsterdam, and about a hundred tents in a magical setting around a lake offer the most unusual and wonderful choice of antiques, bric-a-brac, glassware and flowers. Quite simply to die for.

On the people front, the following designers have also been a major influence on our design decisions: Frederique Mechiche, André Putnam, Caroline Quartermaine, Tricia Guild, the Bloomsbury Group, Cote Bastide and, of course, Sir Terence Conran.

But with all of this, inspiration is not a literal thing. The merest fleck of peeling paint can be the starting point for a whole theme, or a fragrance can unleash a whole new concept – mere nuggets that bear huge fruit.

a sense of place

In the beginning we said that it was not necessary to live in the country to be a subscriber to New Country style and this is most certainly true – for the secret as ever, as with all design directions, is to take elements of the style and match them with what is on offer and what pleases you. New Country makes this easier as it is a relaxed discipline, where the boundaries are undoubtedly blurred and the simplistic angle allows you to add just a few simple touches to make the atmosphere romantic or elegant. However, it goes without saying that your location and the landscape should give you some clues as to where to start on the great decorating plan.

Play to your strengths and let your surroundings suggest a color palette and style. Use local materials to provide tone and texture and don't mask what is naturally provided – enhance it. A touch of whimsy always adds an individual note, such as these colored feathers tied together and placed in a pot, or the graphic statement made by these carved wooden letters, made out of medium density fiberboard and suitably painted and aged.

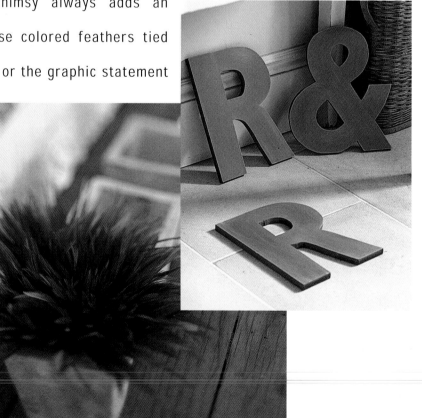

a sense of seasons

In the country, the changing seasons are all the more evident, from the very first shoots of spring flowers in the woodlands to the harvesting of crops in preparation for the long winter months. We make the 100-mile trek to London three times a week, and over the span of a year the countryside provides an ever-changing palette of color that is remarkable. The fields of rape, an intense sulphur-yellow in spring, are followed by cool, calming lavender-blue carpets of flax in early summer. Then the long evenings draw to a close with warm red poppies making way for the gray-greens of winter that turn alpine-white on cold frosty mornings, glistening with jewels. These then are the clear markers for changes in your home – your mood changes as the seasons emerge.

the circle of life

Spring is a delicate time and a time for renewal. The spirits lift with a sense of anticipation, and change is much desired – spring cleaning becomes a therapeutic task. Now is the time to discard the heavy winter drapes and fabrics in favor of lighter, brighter, whiter shades and fill the house with spring bulbs and tiny flowers. Now is the time to rejuvenate tired paintwork or tackle those other decorating tasks you've avoided, so you can reap the benefit during the warmer months.

At Easter, the mood gathers pace as we look forward to the freedom of outdoor living. As the days get longer the light gets stronger and the weather a little kinder – mentally we start to relax and plan days in the garden and meals alfresco. The change in climate makes a dramatic difference to the way we feel, so as your spirits rise in the summer, let the home take on a holiday feel and simplify your surroundings. Make the most of it, for all too soon it vanishes.

Colors change, the harvests are gathered and the new school year signifies the time for life to revert indoors as autumn approaches. It is a time of celebration and festivals and city life heats up again. The autumn is a time of planning and organization and good storage becomes a necessity as you replace your summer trappings with cozier and more pampering textures. Bedding, throws and cushions are the most obvious places to start.

All too soon the dead of winter is nigh and the season of Christmas is upon us. Days are short and the comforts of home are all the more appealing – nature hibernates and so should you. Home becomes a refuge and there is nothing finer than curling up under blankets in front of a roaring fire or taking a long hot and relaxing bath by candlelight. Activities move indoors, so now is the time to fill the home with spicy winter aromas. After the New Year, that spirit of new beginnings returns once more and the whole cycle gets ready to roll all over again.

spring

spring awakening

Spring is a delicate time when Nature gives birth and the countryside is rejuvenated by tiny new blooms. Reflect this by decorating your home with small bunches of simple fresh flowers, such as daffodils, early tulips or violets, or single stems in small bottles. Traditionally forced bulbs like hyacinths never fail to please, whether presented in these special glass vases or more rustic containers like enamel mugs or jam jars. As Easter approaches, add a more whimsical touch by using white feathers either in a wreath or in bowls, and of course make use of plenty of painted eggs, or for a more natural touch try blown quails' eggs. Spring is also the first sign that summer is on its way and your thoughts should turn to outdoor living – now is the time to prepare your garden for the warmer months ahead. Keep an eye open for junk shop finds so you can accessorize and furnish your outdoor space originally.

The palest lemon yellow of primroses is a sure sign that spring has arrived. Used as stems or small bunches in simple containers, they bring an instant freshness and sense of optimism to your room.

The pale yellow theme is picked up by this bowl and square plate. The curvy shapes add a real touch of modernity, yet complement the thick Italian white dish below and the thrush egg blue of the table.

Festoon your kitchen and
dining tables with sprigs of
spring flowers and greenery
for that fresh, spring-is-a-
coming-in atmosphere.

This Chinese plate and bowl are
part of a large set bought in a
market in Hong Kong and carried
lovingly home more than ten
years ago.

let the
sun
shine in

A delightfully simple pair of banner curtains made from chess silk bordered with raw bleached silk makes a striking light filter that doubles as an intriguing, subtle window covering. Simple metal poles fixed to the window frame form a pivoting bracket that acts like a shutter, allowing you to modulate the light to suit your mood, the time of day and the changing seasons.

dream catcher blind

Bringing natural materials into the home is one way of harnessing specific elements so you can appreciate and respect the seasonal changes that surround you. This rich Holland linen banner curtain is inspired by Native American dream catchers, whose spiritual significance is bound up with landscape and the natural world.

1 Choose fabrics with interesting, earthy textures in plain colors. These blinds were made from a wonderful polished Holland linen whose fairly stiff, close-textured weave provides a soft, waxy surface sheen. Measure the size of panels you require to fit your window, allow an extra 1in (25mm) all round the fabric for seams, plus fabric at the top to make a channel for the curtain pole.

2 Mark a rectangle at the required height on the fabric using a set square, ruler and marker pen. Snip the opening and cut tiny nicks at each corner of the rectangle. Fold back the edges to the wrong side, and iron into place. Machine sew all hems, then add one small triangle of fabric at each corner of the opening, so that when light shines through the blinds, a neat edging appears.

3 At the top of the blind fold over the excess fabric to the wrong side and stitch in place, leaving an opening at either end just wide enough to slot over your curtain pole. Finish off the blinds by tying a small feather in the center of each rectangular opening and then stitching a strip of rich brown pheasant feathers along the bottom edge of each panel for soft, textural punctuation.

s u m m e r

summer living

Eating alfresco is a special treat, and as evening falls we place tea-lights (candles) in a variety of containers so they sparkle magically as it gets darker. These pretty Moroccan glasses make ideal candleholders. The large hurricane lamp doubles as a vase, while the other lantern is filled with juniper berries as an attractive base around the candle. To maximize the light in our sitting room (see the following pages), we have discarded our old inherited heavy winter drapes and replaced them with almost sheer, light calico-cotton panels, hemmed at both ends and simply tied to the curtain pole with garden string. Our old faithful wicker chairs have had a facelift by being recovered in a remnant of a pretty jacquard-type cotton, which has an embossed floral print in the weave. The chairs have also been moved much closer to the French doors – a perfect spot to retreat from the summer heat or take an aperitif in the cooler evening air. The boundaries between in and out have been merged by placing an old garden table and a small assembly of pots just inside the doors.

Junk shop finds make essential garden furniture. There is nothing new or brash here, just items that are eclectic, interesting and, above all, fun.

Above, jugs of home-made lemonade are a perfect refreshment for a hot summer's afternoon; whereas, to the right, a freshly-picked flower sits, coolly serene, in an old specimen jar in a quiet corner.

An old French table and planter, bottomless Dutch milk bottles that make wonderful lanterns and wine drunk from bistro-style utility glasses – that and an abundance of fresh air is our idea of heaven. To the left, a generously proportioned chair looks invitingly comfortable for a summer siesta.

bottle stem vases

Never has there been a project where the combination of a few household items transposes more evidently into a piece so pleasing and modern that it could happily sit Hirst-like in a gallery rather than in a relaxed home. Here, a simple broom holder and a milk bottle (admittedly Dutch), combine to elevate themselves into a new dimension. A nicely shaped bottle is the key; try sourcing European mineral waters, bitter Italian drinks or chocolate milk.

1 Cut a piece of ½in (12mm) medium density fiberboard (MDF) to approximately 16in (40cm) square. Stain with water-based woodstain (we have used medium) to enrich the tone, elements of which will show through the paint later in the procedure. Allow to dry (approximately one hour), then seal with acrylic dead-flat (satin) varnish.

2 Paint with two coats of water-based paint (here we have used the colors Mole and Stone), allowing each coat to dry thoroughly. Then gently sand the edges to create a hint of age and provide texture and interest to the board. Once more, seal with a coat of acrylic dead-flat (satin) varnish.

3 Take a metal broom-holder and fix it to just below the middle of the painted and varnished board (you will need to leave sufficient height for the stems of your chosen flowers). Once secure, insert the neck of the bottle into grip of the metal broom-holder and hey! – instant modern art.

kandelini

This project was originally created for a Christmas feature in a magazine and, as usual, because of long lead times, it was shot in the blustery heat of July. However, these mini glass lanterns, inspired by Greek *kandelini*, give a magical touch to a warm summer's evening and make a simple meal alfresco, a divine celebration. String them from branches of trees in clusters, or in porches and doorways or simply on a string across the table. The glass jars are from French yogurts or desserts and are available from speciality food stores.

1 Try to find as many interesting glass pots as you can. We have used lots of French yogurt pots but any similar small glass jars would be fine. Soak the pots in warm soapy water for a few minutes to remove any labels, then wash and dry them thoroughly before use.

2 Cut fine-guage wire into 4in (10cm) and 20in (50cm) strips and then use long-nose pliers to create a small loop at one end of each of the shorter pieces of wire. For each jar, thread a longer wire through the loops of two shorter pieces of wire to create a noose.

3 Sharply pull the noose tight around the neck of the yogurt pot and twist the ends together, so that the wire sits securely under the rim. When hanging in the desired location, just twist together the ends of the wires to secure the lantern in place.

autumn

autumn textures

As the nights draw in it's time to cozy-up a little for the cooler months ahead. More than any other season, autumn is all about texture. As with your clothes, it's time for those light floaty fabrics to be stowed away and replaced with warmer woolen throws and blankets, comforting cushions and rugs.

Create autumnal still lifes from nature's gifts; choose interesting seed heads from dried flowers and combine them with an ever-changing foliage of autumn fruits and nuts. Acorns and pine cones are to autumn what pebbles and shells are to summer. Take tea by the fireside and light candles as early evening approaches – at this time of year the flickering light provides warmth as well as a magical quality. Enhance this with incense in woody or spicy fragrances like cedar and vanilla.

To the right, these floating
candles look beautiful in the
glass votives of this modern take
on a chandelier – a veritable
pyramid of light. Below, a pillar
candle burns steadily and evenly
while giving off the citrus notes
of winter fruits. Only a real log
fire will do in the country and
dried herbs like sage make
wonderful aromatic kindling or
can create great aromas when
sprinkled on the embers of a fire.

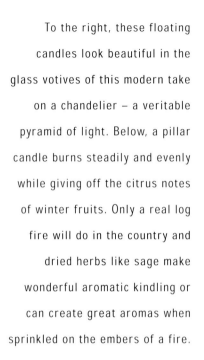

We call these oddities leaf sconces because of the handsome rusty metal leaf that forms each holder. The flames of the tea-lights look stunning as they are reflected in the ripple of the utilitarian glass. Below, a touch of glamour is added to these metal votives by the addition of myriad tiny glass beads.

golden brown

It is surprising that many people do not know how relatively easy it is to create a waxed finish on a piece of furniture. Here we show you a more unusual darker waxing that emulates exotic hardwoods using humble white pine. The darker finish also picks up on the big influx into modern interiors of dark wood with a hint of the east, and is perfect for dining tables or for re-creating thirties retro-style furniture like desks or chests.

1 Use a dark shade of water-based woodstain (here we have used a walnut effect) and apply carefully with a brush along the grain of the wood. Work quickly and keep a wet edge going at all times. Take care not to overlap the woodstain too much at the edges to avoid a build up of color. Repeat if necessary.

2 Apply a coat of furniture wax, either clear or antique pine. Use a soft cloth or medium grade wire wool to apply the wax evenly and quickly and again be careful on those edges. Allow to dry thoroughly for at least one hour – when dry the wax will have virtually disappeared into the wood.

3 Polish and buff the surface to a sheen using a clean, dry soft cloth. Always use a toluene-free wax as it is less toxic and, usually, has a slightly less glossy sheen to the finished result. For the desk, we also stained and waxed the drawers and, to complete the retro look, added an antiqued drawer pull.

the matador chair

Sexy or what? This chair cover was inspired by furniture we discovered in a swanky bar in Brussels. This was not its original purpose, but it is undoubtedly a great way to transform an old chair past its sell-by date – terrific as a stand-alone piece, and equally stunning used in combination with other chairs around a dining table.

1 Create a more shapely, upholstered look by giving the chair shoulder pads. Cut a piece of foam the width and thickness of the top of the chair back and secure in place with masking tape. Measure the width of the seat and back to calculate the width of the large fabric panel required to go from the bottom of the chair back to the front of the legs. Allow ¼in (5mm) on each side for seams.

2 Lay the chair on a large piece of paper, such as lining paper, and draw around the outline to create a pattern for the side panels. Again, allow an extra ¼in (5mm) for the seams. Cut out the side panels for the chair cover using these templates, then use the same templates to calculate how long the main flat panel of fabric for the chair seat and back needs to be.

3 Thankfully, ready-made piping is now widely available, as is a plethora of wonderful trimmings; here a pom-pom fringe adds a whimsical touch to a fairly formal design. Insert the piping between the panel and side seams, then pin and sew together to make the cover. Fold up the bottom. Press and pin the fringe in place; it may be easier to hand sew the fringe due to the thickness of the combined materials.

winter

winter festivals

The winter season is a busy one with more celebrations and festivals than any other time of year, but it is these gatherings that lift the spirits and brighten up the long, dark and despairingly dull days. At these times, the comfort of home makes it all too difficult to leave the nest.

Fire and light play a huge part at this time of year. There is nothing finer than the crackle and snap and the unique aroma of a real log fire, providing warmth, energy and soul to a home. In the country, where log burning is much more common, the night air is literally filled with a smoky incense that is very becoming.

For lighting, use lamps to create pools of interest and welcoming light rather than overhead ambient lighting, and further enhance the atmosphere with living lights in the form of candles or little tea-lights. A single candle on a table over supper will add such spirit that even the humblest meal will be transformed; a lantern in the window will provide a warm welcome to friends and family, and a scented candle like cinnamon or fennel will emanate sweet undertones that are instantly uplifting.

MERYL

JOYEUX NOEL!

A festive still-life awaits visitors as they arrive in our small hallway – the huge silver ball adding a restrained glamour to the proceedings, the fresh flowers a sense of occasion.

Above, you see the contemporary wire Christmas tree with its burning votives and a favorite card to symbolize the spirit of giving and receiving (this one is by artist friend Lydia Bates).

To the left, presents are wrapped in simple plain papers and enhanced with ribbons and natural decorations; sprigs of rosemary are loosely fitted inside the bows. Below, champagne sunk into an old galvanized tub filled with ice sits comfortably with the elegance of the glass chandelier behind – both providing the celebratory touch.

Below, the Christmas table is laid with welcoming goodie bags and individual placenames, with holly and rosemary at each place.

TIGGY

JOYEUX NOEL!

table
talk

Rather than expensive and lavish and gifts, it's the little touches at Christmas that make others feel so special. The computer age has meant that we can all readily print invitations and name cards easily, so keep a look out for interesting papers to print on. We used a beautifully frosty-looking thick tracing paper that perfectly matched the little hand-sewn organdy bags that we put at each place setting. We filled these with amaretti and small silver cake decorations for a touch of festive sparkle.

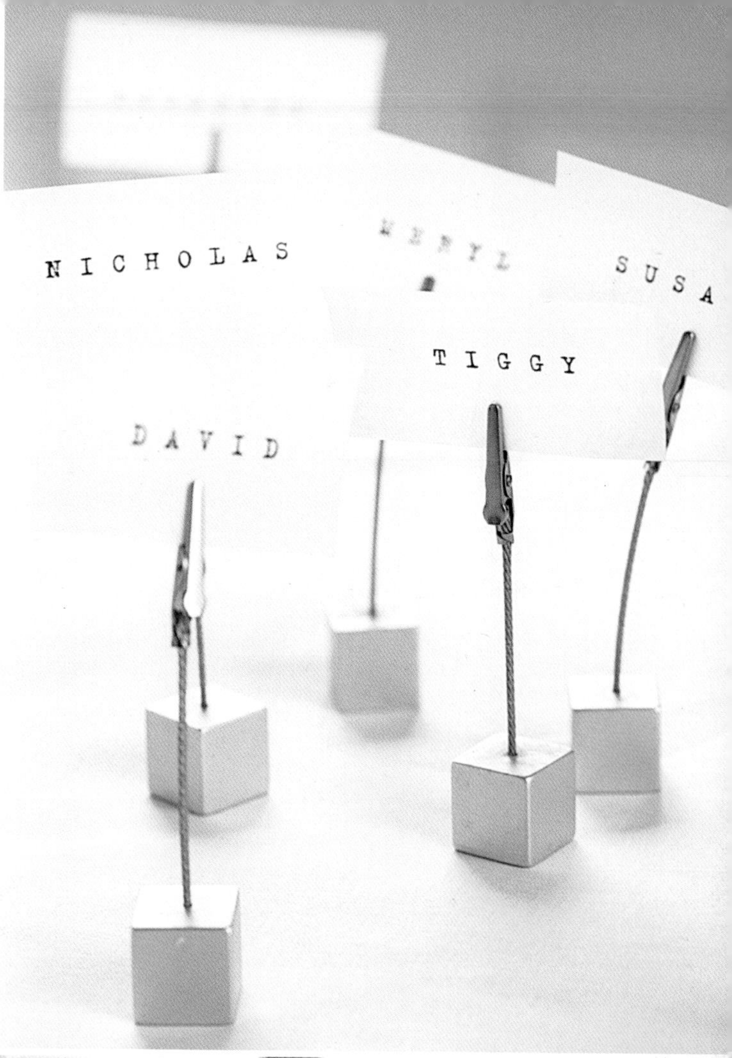

NICHOLAS

TIGGY

SUSA

DAVID

JOYEUX NOEL!

HAPPY CHRISTMAS!

Winter textures are all around us, from nature's natural patterned coil, to the weave of the throw and to the amazingly real-looking bloom of the faux suede table cover that is pictured opposite.

Throws are amazingly versatile. Use them on chairs, sofas or beds and both as decorative features and as winter warmers to keep those toes cozy.

Enjoy such simple textural contrasts as this smooth sofa cover beneath a woolen sweater or the faux suede table cover in front of a pile of logs, ready for burning in that fireplace.

the square set

Metallic paints are making a comeback and bear little resemblance to their eighties forerunner Hammerite. Now they can even be water-based and offer a variety of naturalistic finishes. Used in moderation they can enhance a colorwashed wall and should certainly be considered by those who lean towards modernity.

1 Paint the wall with a pale gray emulsion (latex). A true emulsion is essential for a good colorwash base as it is packed with plastic and so less porous than our own water-based paint, allowing the wash to move and spread when applied. We then created a wash from our chalky Elephant Grey diluted five times with water and mixed well. Apply in haphazard brushstrokes then rag-in and soften with a clean, dry soft cloth.

2 Allow the wash to dry then mark a vertical guideline on the wall with a spirit level and tailor's chalk to use as the starting point for creating a repeat. Cut a square cardboard template to the distance between repeats, in our case 12in (30cm). Place two corners of the template on the guideline and mark the other corners. Move it around, marking as you go, always with two corners on previously made marks.

3 Cut a kitchen sponge into a square with a scalpel and then use the sponge as your stamp to imprint the metallic squares on to the wall using the repeat marks as your guide. The sponge provides a nice textured pattern but always try it first on some scrap card before tackling the wall. You'll find that a mini-roller is useful to keep the paint even in the plate or tray.

a distressing affair

To this very day, this is one of our favorite techniques for giving an instant 'aged' and careworn appearance to otherwise fairly mundane and soul-less pieces. The same method can be used to give an ultra-distressed look to furniture, although care should be taken not to overdo the effect!

1 Stain the frames with a water-based woodstain (here we used medium) and allow to dry. Seal the stain with either shellac sanding sealer or acrylic dead-flat (satin) varnish. If using this technique on furniture, use shellac as it will seal the knots as well. When using shellac, clean brushes in methylated spirits and do not pour any excess into the sink as it solidifies when in contact with water.

2 Use a rubber solution fabric glue or artist's masking fluid for this step and paint on irregular, haphazard patches in places where you want the wood to show through. Take care not to be too symmetrical in your aging and distressing technique, ensuring that your masking reflects the jagged edges of naturally peeling paint – actually far easier than it sounds.

3 When the glue is dry and transparent (about 30 minutes), paint the frames with two coats of water-based paint (we used Chalk), allowing each coat to dry before applying the next. Gently rub back the edges with medium sandpaper allowing the glue to be revealed. Then carefully pull off the glue to leave jagged patches where the paint has supposedly peeled with age. Clean and seal with two coats of varnish.

a place at the table

The country kitchen, with its potent mix of comfort, familiarity and sustenance is always at the emotional heart of a rural home. Once a place where everything was slightly too threadbare, it has evolved into a room of restrained elegance and practicality. At once informal and inviting, clean-lined yet lived in, the New Country kitchen is a place where good eating, easy living and a sense of calm are all-embracing – a meeting place where friends gather, plans are made and meals are treasured in an atmosphere that revitalizes you from day to day. Getting the look is all about searching through your visual dictionary, developing an appreciation of the simple things in life and being willing to seek out the unexpected.

a restraining order

A New Country kitchen is likely to be a collection of unfitted pieces rather than anything fitted or formal – a place where sleek tiling will sit happily with old faucets, counters and dressers and modernity will spring from containers and stainless steel pans, with appliances once again becoming a feature rather than being something to be hidden away. However, the whole concept of storage and display needs to be given great thought. Invariably a compromise will be reached – after all, while it is most modern to suggest that fitted cupboards are past their sell-by date, open shelving attracts dust, and not all foodstuffs carry attractive labels and come in shapes that have visual appeal.

Similarly, the food that is prepared is likely to be unfussy and seasonal. Our food culture has become lighter and unstructured, and for almost everyone now, there is a huge choice of organic vegetables and a wide array of fresh salads, fruits and herbs. Make every

evening meal a celebration rather than a chore to get through – unwind, light a candle or tea-light to lift your spirits and create atmosphere, choose varied and interesting breads as an accompaniment to the meal and take a look at how you present the food. There's a wealth of inspiration out there now in the plethora of food magazines and television programs – take from them what you will. The very process of producing food has the power to nurture and restore.

Choose a neutral scheme for the kitchen as this will open up the choice of china and glassware – the days of slavish sophisticated matching have gone. Loosen up and buy individual pieces that inspire you; utility ware can sit happily beside relaxed elegance; indeed, this is a must. Informal gatherings are often the best and a mix-and-match approach will ensure that your kitchen has a carefree feel about it.

home grown

There is something unbelievably satisfying about home-grown produce, whether it is flowers, fruit, vegetables or herbs. Thankfully, you need neither to be an expert nor to have a large garden. A good crop of tomatoes, for example, could be gleaned from say four or five pots, while herbs could be successfully grown in the confines of a window box. Whatever the crop, your efforts will be rewarded by a taste that is sublime and quite apart from that of produce you buy in the supermarket, even organic.

For a really personal touch to a supper party or barbecue, why not create small posies of fresh herbs and put them at each place? Then your guests can add them at random to their salad or supper as the meal progresses. This is a truly delightful gesture that your friends will cherish.

You won't find crystal in our glass cupboard! Just an eclectic assortment of mainly modern glassware. And, left, this old rustic table was given a new lease of life with some chalk-white paint, fairly heavily distressed to preserve the charm.

No home should be without the ubiquitous set of white china – just perfect for casual or sophisticated dining. These inexpensive pieces are made by a small family firm in Italy. Wonderfully heavy and chunky, they feel so generous. And, right, bruschetta, a simple Italian snack that is to die for – sprinkle with olive oil and salt and you're in heaven!

breakfast for friends

There is nothing more luxurious than a leisurely breakfast, and a lazy relaxed one shared with friends is a joy to be savored. As with lunch or dinner, presentation is all-important, in an informal way – a selection of platters and baskets on a side table would lend itself to this, especially as arrival times at table are likely to be staggered. Not everyone works at the same pace in the mornings, so be prepared to be flexible. In winter, start the meal with a hearty bowl of oatmeal, followed by an interesting basket of assorted toasted breads and home-made jams. In summer, go for a lighter touch and follow the Dutch for inspiration. Offer a mixture of ham and milky cheeses, hard-boiled eggs and again the basket of warmed breads – all washed down with gallons of freshly-brewed coffee or tea. Without doubt though, a good leisurely breakfast is a special treat, and with friends a time of intimacy, exploration and discovery as you plan the day ahead. So sit back, eat and enjoy!

This old chandelier was inherited with the house and is a focal point for the room, sitting comfortably with the vaguely modern decor. For the most part, we keep the blind neatly rolled and save the loose swags (see page 97) for celebrations. Above right, incense provides a delightful woody undertone when fragrancing a room.

Use nature to provide little details and decorations. The twigs to the left blend naturally with the neutral tones of the china, and contrast with the napkin and the dark wood below.

Stems of dried seeds also make an interesting and modern table decoration in narrow glass vases. Used singly or in groups of twos or threes they remain sufficiently unobtrusive in the middle of the dining table.

bloomsbury frieze

Although we're not the greatest fans of stenciling, we do occasionally like to use rubber stamps. They give you the freedom to create pattern repeats that look believably professional. While commercially bought stamps are fine, making your own by the method shown here gives you the freedom to express yourself and create beautiful patterns that have a more painterly quality.

1 Use a pencil and an artist's curve to draw the leaf design onto a computer mouse mat and then use a scalpel to carefully cut out the leaves and the stem. With rubber solution fabric glue, stick the cut-out shapes top-side down onto a small piece of medium density fiberboard (MDF) so that the foam side of the mouse mat is visible .

2 Around the top of the wall at the height you wish the frieze to sit, mark a base line using a spirit level and tailor's chalk. Put water-based paint in a dish or tray (here we have used French Grey) and apply evenly to the leaf stamp with a mini-roller. Repeat each time you stamp. For corners, stamp the design onto card and use as a stencil, completing the design freehand.

3 We actually made three stamps – a left and right spray and a small simple stem shape for the central image to hold it all together. Use wooden knobs screwed into the back of the boards to provide a useful handle for the stamp. If creating a small single motif or pattern, you could glue the rubber matting directly to the base of large wooden knobs available in hardware stores.

window dressing

In a chapter dedicated to the culinary side of life it is eminently suitable to refer to this window treatment as a dressing. While entirely practical and workable in itself, it also enhances the bulk-standard roller blind with which it is combined, to make an elegant yet simple statement fit to adorn any window.

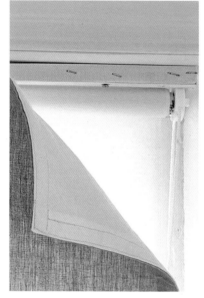

1 Measure the width and length of your windows and cut two panels of fabric to fit – we have used a natural linen for the front and a white cotton for the lining. Allow an extra ¼in (5mm) on each side for the hems and sew the panels together, right sides facing and then turn through. Cut, sew and press four 4¾in- (12cm-) wide strips of the linen approximately one and a half times the length of the blind, to act as the ties.

2 Hang a simple and plain roller blind, according to the manufacturer's instructions, at the back of the window and then use screws to fix a small batten of wood across the top of the window frame just in front of the roller blind. Using a staple gun or glue, fix one half of a single strip of Velcro across the wooden batten which will be used to fix the window dressing.

3 Sew two ties to the top of each side of the blind and the other half of the Velcro all across the top seam – use this Velcro strip to attach the blind to the wooden batten. Gently gather up the blind in loose folds to the required height and then tie the bows to keep it in place. For a simpler, less swag-like appearance, roll up the blind instead of gathering it.

sleep and dreams

There is no room in the house more deserving of being a haven of sensuality than the bedroom – probably the most private of rooms and where each of us escapes daily for replenishment and rest. It is therefore essential to decorate it in a style that makes you feel relaxed and pampered; the room should be filled with your favorite things. Marcel Proust wrote: 'sleep surrounds the lives of men as the sea surrounds a peninsula'. This is a perfect analogy, for it is the restful decor, the choice of soothing color and the thoughtful little touches that are conducive to that state of well-being that comes from a really good night's sleep. So go on ... pamper yourself with soothing colors and make your peninsula a special place.

rest and relaxation

A bedroom can be part boudoir, part dressing room, part sitting room but above all it is a room that should make you feel happy and relaxed. The bed will no doubt be the focal point and it is imperative that you choose a good one, not just for its looks but for comfort – not too hard and not too soft. Think of it as a headland caressed by the sea.

Use sheer fabrics to create minimal window treatments rather than drown your windows with heavy drapes – the sheers provide privacy yet have a dreamlike quality that allows maximum light. Choose soothing pastel colors for the walls rather than invigorating stronger colors, and for a touch of luxury layer the bed with a variety of fabrics, pillows and throws for softness and texture. Use wool and mohair blankets and feather-filled quilts generously folded in winter and replaced in the summer by lighter, crisper cottons and linens with transparent organdy or embroidered pillowcases.

To get a good night's sleep, ensure that you have a constant flow of fresh air. There's nothing like a hot bath for relieving the tensions of the day – make it just long enough and hot enough to relax those tired muscles, and a glass of milk will help you unwind. Try a few simple relaxation exercises – gently turn your head from left to right several times to relax the neck muscles, slowly stretch your arms and exercise your wrist and fingers.

Prepare your dreams in advance – imagine what you'd like to be or do if you were completely free; this is your chance for pure escapism. Be a navigator and decide upon a direction; determine what you will say or do tomorrow to resolve a particular problem, and if you still cannot sleep, rather than counting sheep, try counting waves breaking on the beach. For those with stress in their lives, there is no doubt that a night's sleep will aid perspective. Replenishment is vital, so sleep well on your peninsula.

We mixed fabric paint to match
the bed and painted a border onto
this cotton voile and suspended it
from two dowel rods just hung off
small hooks fixed in the ceiling
for an instant canopy. The real
antique pine gives the room an
Alpine feel.

In the cooler months add warmth
and luxury with an assortment
of textured throws and blankets.
We added a touch of whimsy by
using these faux fur cushions,
which were available in our
local department store and
amazingly inexpensive.

To complete the Alpine look, we
embroidered loose star shapes at
random on to simple white cotton
sheets. These add a crisp clean
definition to the soft gray jersey
duvet cover and beautiful woolen
star blanket.

guests and visitors

To invite guests for the weekend is a very personal gesture; it can be daunting that these people are going to see you for more than just a few hours, warts and all. Some people are natural experts as weekend hosts. The key to a successful visit is to make guests at ease from the moment they arrive – a little welcoming gift beside the bed, such as a special soap, is a great place to start. Plan lots of activity for the first few hours, maybe a shared task – whatever it is, it'll break down the barriers and lead early on to a relaxed and informal atmosphere. Have a loose agenda, so everyone knows the timetable, and arrange a morning rendezvous. Awaken your guests with a tray of tea accompanied by a small stem of fresh flowers picked from the garden; it's the little touches that make the difference. It may take a lot of time in planning and preparation, but weekends that are shared with friends help create a special bond that will last the test of time.

Lighter summer bedding has replaced the heavier throws of winter and, below, pretty stems are placed in this modern test-tube vase on the rattan butler's tray. The sheers are tied simply with bows of garden twine.

More stems are placed in pretty bottles, and a gorgeously fruity triple-wick candle burns to enhance the summer fragrances blowing in from the garden. To complete the floaty look, pillowcases were made from organdy cotton to preserve the spirit of lightness and dreams.

tension wire four poster

There's something rather nice about being ensconsed in a four poster bed. Use floaty sheer fabrics that allow the light through to bring out the soft, pampering elements of bedtime. The wealth of sheer fabrics around is huge – many stores offer ready-sewn panels. Sheer plain whites are romantic, contemporary and incredibly inexpensive. Tension wire kits are available from department stores.

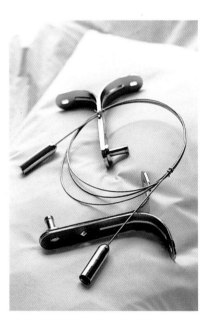

1 Position and fix the wire holders to the ceiling, using a beam or joist for safety and lining them up so the sheers will hang parallel to the edge of the bed. Fix in the wires and tighten so that they become taut.

2 We used commercially available textured sheer panels for the brown curtain and then dyed some inexpensive muslin to make the second curtain. This, of course, had to be hemmed on all sides for a neat finish.

3 Next punch holes into the top hem of the curtains with a bradawl (awl) and tie individual lengths of garden twine through these holes. When the curtains are hung on the taut wire the twine can be tied in bows.

outdoor living

For all of us, it is important to establish a link with nature, no matter how small, and we get that from our gardens or outdoor spaces. These are essential to provide perspective and an anchor to this high-tech society that we live in. The garden or the garden room is a sensual affair too. The texture of the plants and trees, the earthy terracotta pots and the intoxicating smell of summer flowers or aromatic herbs all play their part in minimizing the stresses of the day. This harmony does not necessarily require a large garden. The tiniest backyard, a veranda, a conservatory or city window-boxes are all perfectly capable of providing the necessary essence of outdoor living at its best.

outdoor rooms

The garden or the garden room is as much a part of the home as any other room and should be savored. Tending plants can be therapeutic, and spending quality time in the fresh air a truly revitalizing and healing process.

Whatever the space, treat it in exactly the same way as you design the rest of the house – what are its main purposes, what are its strengths and weaknesses? – and fuse the two by bringing plants in and taking furniture out. French doors are a great translator, perfectly linking one world with another. Go for a relaxed and informal style, just as you have indoors, and add a whimsical touch – architectural antiques make great garden sculptures. Avoid the worst of new garden furniture and go for pieces that have character, an eclectic mix of junk-shop finds, simple tables and café chairs. Decking provides a

masterful solution with its warm and worn structure, perfect for places where space is limited and an ideal platform for a collection of plants in pots.

Lighting is important too – an abundance of candles and tea-lights gives a magical quality to a summer's evening, no table is complete without a glass storm lantern, and the twinkle of fairy lights in a tree or bush adds a touch of glamour that is almost surreal.

There's no doubt that eating alfresco is one of the true delights of summer living – some of our fondest memories are of simple meals outside. Food tastes so much better outdoors; why, even the humble sausage can be elevated to heights never before dreamed of. Above all, though, make the most of your outdoor space, morning, noon and night.

garden pots

As a former dairy, our main garden is more like a secret garden, obscured from view from the house by a collection of outbuildings and an abundance of green shrubbery. So for us it was important to concentrate on creating pretty terraces and patio areas using pots and containers, like this one by the front door. This is essential to provide an interesting landscape and warm welcome to visitors and friends while also providing a sense of order and scale in stark contrast to the rambling garden beyond.

Thankfully, pots are now readily available in all shapes and sizes and are relatively inexpensive – you can create added interest by combining them with architectural antiques like metal urns, orbs and crowns, plus old chairs, steps and other junk-shop finds, which in our case include a magnificent long rusty Dutch lantern. This south-facing spot gets sunshine all day and is therefore the perfect venue for outdoor living. To complete the picture, we've now added a bench and two old lounge chairs salvaged from a French *brocante* (junk yard).

Garden pots do not have to be limited to the terracotta variety. Search out various shapes and materials – here the deep pink geranium is nestling comfortably in a wicker basket.

One of our most successful of garden decorations, this wrought iron crown can be put to good use for plants to trail over and around (see the previous page) or as a decorative device in its own, truly majestic, right.

Don't confine outdoor living to your garden. If you are lucky enough to live near the beach – or choose to holiday on the coast – equip yourself with lamp and windbreak and enjoy some early evenings by the sea. See pages 128-133 for our ideas of a good day out, seaside-wise.

an evening in the garden

As the sun sets on a summer's evening, the garden becomes rather a magical place. The light of dusk takes on a special quality and the flowers and shrubs, their powerful scent still lingering, almost sigh with relief as the heat and action of the day diminish. Remember that feeling of walking barefoot on evening grass and you will know what we mean – soft and sublime.

Enhance this magic by a few simple touches. Light small votives or containers with tea-lights (candles) and dot them around the garden, hang *kandelini* in the trees and bushes like the Greeks (see pages 46-47 for our project) – almost any container will do, the more the merrier. These twinkling, living lights will do more for atmosphere than you could ever imagine. If you're entertaining, light a friendly lantern to welcome guests.

colorwashed chairs

If you take nothing else from this book then take this project. Basic one- and two-color aging has been the cornerstone of our success and has a relevance every bit as much today as ten years ago when the media first started featuring our painted furniture. Slightly worn, slightly faded painted pieces fit very much into the romantic part of the story of interior design – only the colors have changed.

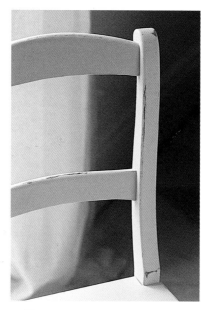

1 If your piece of furniture is new wood then follow the first step on page 77 to seal the wood. If the piece has been waxed you need to remove the wax with methylated spirits and wire wool before sealing with shellac. If your piece has been varnished, simply give it a light sanding to create a key.

2 Apply two coats of water-based paint in your chosen color, allowing each one to dry thoroughly. Then with medium-grade sandpaper, gently sand all over, rubbing harder on the edges, to reveal the wood beneath. Wipe with a dry cloth and seal with two coats of acrylic dead-flat (satin) varnish.

3 To reveal a more dramatic amount of wood, as shown on the sample above, dilute the first coat of paint with roughly 50 per cent water before painting the whole piece. With the second coat, which you use at full strength, paint only areas where you really want solid paint to remain. Sand back and seal as in the previous step.

beach canopy

There's something very pleasing about being under canvas when the sun shines, maybe because it reminds one of those adventures from childhood. This canopy is an elegant alternative to the ubiquitous garden umbrella and one that is vaguely portable (you'll need a roof rack on your car!), delightful to sit under and provides valuable shade from the sun overhead. You might find it more practical to use the canopy within the privacy of your own garden or some other secluded spot.

1 To create the supports for the canopy, cut four 1½in (40mm) diameter bamboo poles into 2½yd (2.3m) lengths with a hand saw. Although we have used bamboo here, poles made from any treated sawn timber would make equally good supports.

2 Cut a piece of canvas to roughly 2½ x 1¾yd (2.3 x 1.6m) and hem all the edges. To reinforce the corners, use leather arm patches that have been cut in half, folded in two and then sewn over the canvas. Next use an eyelet kit to create the metal rings, which are positioned over each reinforced corner.

3 Using a bradawl (awl), make a small hole about 4in (10cm) down the pole and fix a large brass hook securely in place. To erect, hang the canopy on the hooks and sink the poles deep into the sand or earth. Make taut with tie-ropes from the poles to smaller battens, which are also sunk into the ground.

windbreaker

Here's another very simple project that makes a trip to the beach a little more stylish. Beach equipment is, of course, readily available in any seaside town but the fabrics used tend to be garish and bright. So why not customize your own? We used a nautical looking dark blue check, but a pretty floral number would look equally smart – although possibly not for the men. Also in the photograph opposite you'll see our handy beach bed. Buy three squares of foam and make cotton covers as you would for a cushion and string them together with tape. What could be simpler?

1 For the windbreaker, take four broom handles or dowel rods and stain them with water-based woodstain (we have used medium).

2 Choose 3¼yd (3m) of a suitable fabric – we have used a heavy cotton that measures 36in (90cm) wide so no hemming was required.

3 At both ends and at 1yd (1m) intervals, pin and sew channels in the fabric so the poles slide in place and the fabric fits snugly around them.

new country palette

Throughout this book we've used a paler palette than ever before – all the colors were designed to be balanced and uplifting. They are contemporary yet hint at a faded past. French Grey and Mole are traditional furniture colors in France, yet when used on a wall and combined with dark furniture, they speak every inch of modernity. Parchment offers a softer alternative to white and is perfect for woodwork. It also works well with Chalk and Stone – our biggest sellers. Mulberry Fool and Periwinkle Blue are very pretty colors; Tourmaline has a fifties quality, and Chinese Leaf and Parma Violet have an invigorating freshness. All these shades are perfect for the current light floral revival.

materials & techniques

It is our heartfelt belief that all the projects featured in *New Country Decorating* are easy to achieve and the results convincingly professional. All the materials used are readily available from hardware or department stores.

The color references and paints used throughout this book are based on our own range of Traditional Paints, shown in their entirety on the following pages. Water-based, they emulate the milk paints of the nineteenth century and are similar to an acrylic distemper – chalky and flat. This makes them perfect for techniques that require aging or rubbing-back. They are fine for wood and walls alike, except that care should be taken with the

darker colors when used on large flat surfaces, as they mark easily. We recommend that they be finished with a final coat of acrylic dead-flat (satin) varnish. Other hand-made paints should perform in a similar manner. Regular vinyl emulsion (latex) paint is, of course, fine for walls and also colorwashing.

If you use our paints for colorwashing, we suggest you use them for the wash only and not the base coat. If you need to make the walls wipeable, then you will need to seal them with a coat of acrylic dead-flat (satin) varnish, taking great care not to brush off the wash as you apply the varnish – spraying the wall with artist's fixative first will help.

paint swatches

Traditional Palette

109 Buttermilk

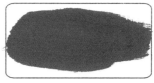
111 Caspian Blue

522 Apple Green

130 Mocha

119 Gustavian Blue

622 Blush

106 Cayenne

104 Providence Blue

120 Eau de Nil

114 Cranberry

107 Chalk

117 Sorrel

116 Poppy

621 Pistachio

118 Elephant Grey

526 Duck Egg Blue

625 Shutter Green

108 Bayberry

132 Stockholm Blue

623 Antique Lime

Country Living Palette

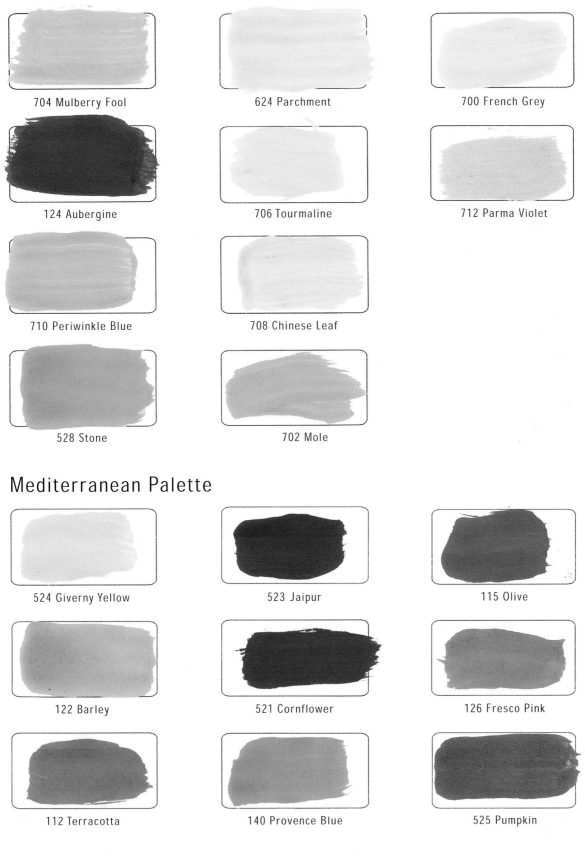

704 Mulberry Fool

624 Parchment

700 French Grey

124 Aubergine

706 Tourmaline

712 Parma Violet

710 Periwinkle Blue

708 Chinese Leaf

528 Stone

702 Mole

Mediterranean Palette

524 Giverny Yellow

523 Jaipur

115 Olive

122 Barley

521 Cornflower

126 Fresco Pink

112 Terracotta

140 Provence Blue

525 Pumpkin

suppliers

US suppliers in italics

Paints and varnishes

Grand Illusions
Mail order
PO Box 81
Shaftesbury
Dorset SP7 8TA
UK
Tel: +44 1747 854092

Grand Illusions
2-4 Crown Road
St Margarets
Twickenham
Middlesex TW1 3EE
UK
Tel: +44 20 8607 9446

Grand Illusions
118 Walcot Street
Bath
Avon BA1 5BG
UK
Tel: +44 1225 427284

Colourman Paints
Stockingate
Coton Clanford
Stafford ST18 9PB
UK
Tel: +44 1785 282799

Craig and Rose plc
172 Leith Walk
Edinburgh EH6 5ER
UK
Tel: +44 131 554 1131

Paint Magic
116 Sheen Road
Richmond
Surrey TW9 1UR
UK
Tel: +44 20 8940 9799

Relics of Witney
35 Bridge Street
Witney
Oxon OX8 6DA
UK
Tel: +44 1993 704611

Createx Colors
14 Airport Park Road
East Granby, CT 06026
Tel: (800) 243 2712

Old-Fashioned Milk Paint Company
PO Box 22
Grolon, MA 01450
Tel: (617) 448 6336

Paint Effects
2426 Fillmore Street
San Francisco, CA 94115
Tel: (415) 292 7780

General

B&Q
Branches throughout the UK
Phone for your nearest branch
Tel: +44 2380 256256

Homebase
Branches throughout the UK
Phone for your nearest branch
Tel: +44 20 8784 7200

IKEA
Branches throughout the UK
Phone for your nearest branch
Tel: +44 20 8208 5600

Jerry's Home Store
163-167 Fulham Road
London SW3 6FN
UK
Tel: +44 20 7581 0909

John Lewis Partnership
Branches throughout the UK
Phone for your nearest branch
Tel: +44 7828 1000

Muji
187 Oxford Street
London W1R 1AG
UK
Tel: +44 20 7437 7503

Paperchase
213-215 Tottenham Court Road
London W1P 9AF
UK
Tel: +44 20 7467 6200

Paperchase
92 Victoria Street
London SW1E
UK
+44 7828 6458

The Conran Shop
81 Fulham Road
London SW3 6RD
UK
Tel: +44 20 7589 7401

Chaselle Inc
9645 Gerwig Lane
Columbia, MD 21046
Tel: (800) 242 7355

IKEA
1000 Center Drive
Elizabeth, NJ 07202
Tel: (908) 289 4488

The Artist's Club
5750 N.E. Hassalo
Portland, OR 97213
Tel: (800) 845 6507

Second-hand furniture/antiques

After Noah
121 Upper Street
Islington
London N1 1QP
UK
Tel: +44 20 7359 4281

After Noah
261 Kings Road
Chelsea
London SW3 5EL
UK
Tel: +44 20 7351 2610

Castle Gibson
106a Upper Street
Islington
London N1 1QN
UK
Tel: +44 20 7704 0927

Decorative Living
55 New Kings Road
Chelsea
London SW6 4SE
UK
Tel: +44 20 7736 5623

Source
93-95 Walcot Street
Bath
Avon BA1 5BG
UK
Tel: +44 1225 469200

Walcot Reclamation
108 Walcot Street
Bath
Avon BA1 5BG
UK
Tel: +44 1225 444404

Fabrics

Designer's Guild
Mail order
PO Box 5050
Annesley
Nottingham NG15 0DL
UK
Tel: +44 845 602 1189

Designers Guild
267-271 & 275-277 Kings Road
Chelsea
London SW3 5EN
UK
Tel: +44 20 7351 5775

Cath Kidston
Mail order
115 Clarendon Road
Notting Hill
London W11 4JG
UK
Tel: +44 20 7229 8000

Cath Kidston
8 Clarendon Cross
Notting Hill
London W11 4AP
UK
Tel: +44 20 7221 4000

Ian Mankin
109 Regents Park Road
London NW1 8UR
UK
Tel: +44 20 7722 0997

Russell & Chapple
68 Drury Lane
Covent Garden
London WC2B 5SP
UK
Tel: +44 20 7836 7521

Whaley's
Harris Court
Great Horton
Bradford BD7 4EQ
UK
Tel: +44 1274 576718

Coconut Company
129-131 Greene Street
New York, NY 10012
Tel: (212) 539 1940

Homespun Fabrics and Draperies
PO Box 3223
Ventura, CA 93006
Tel: (805) 642 8111

Natural Fiber Fabric Club
PO Box 1115
Mountainside, NJ 07092

acknowledgments

We would like to thank the following people for their enormous help in the production of this book:

Denise Bates at Ebury Press for her continuing support and trust in us and, on this occasion, her enduring patience. Emma Callery, a generous and supportive editor and Alison Shackleton for her contribution to the layouts and design.

Our three wonderful and superbly talented photographers David Downie, Andrew Wood and Caroline Arber – it has been such a pleasure, even though the stress at times was enormous.

To all our staff, past and present, both in London and Dorset, whose daily contribution makes the whole thing tick, and without whose help it would not be possible. Chris Mowe, for continuing to make such brilliant paint, and whose guidance and inspiration changed our lives forever.

To all our customers, industry colleagues, journalists, friends and family – your warmth and generosity continues to motivate and inspire us – may that never end.

Special thanks to Jonathan Ronald, Susan Vickerman and Tiggs for being there when we needed you.

Lastly, our very dear friends and mentors – Meryl Lloyd and Joanna Copestick, two remarkable women who have such faith in us and offer unstinting generosity – we shall be forever grateful.

index